# The Case of the Missing Homework

Leslie Arnott

Illustrated by K.E. Lewis

## Rigby
A Harcourt Achieve Imprint

www.Rigby.com
1-800-531-5015

Nina sat in the kitchen and
did her homework.
Her little sister Sophia watched.

"I want to do homework, too,"
said Sophia.

"You're not old enough," said Nina,
"but you can draw."

Sophia's eyes lit up.

She drew a picture for Nina,

and Nina worked on her homework.

After they were done working,
Nina hung up Sophia's picture.

The next morning, Nina got ready for school.

She packed her books in her bag, but her homework was missing.

Nina looked around the kitchen,
but she didn't find it there.

Then Nina checked around Dad's big brown chair, but she didn't find it there.

Next she checked the toy chest
in her bedroom.
She still didn't find her homework.

The morning was growing old.
She would have to leave
for school soon.

What was she going to do?

Just then Sophia ran into the room.
She stopped when she saw Nina.
"Are you ok?" she asked.

"My homework is missing,"
Nina said.

"Come with me," Sophia said.

She took Nina back to the kitchen.

"It's right there," she said.

"That's your picture," said Nina.

"I drew it on the back of your homework," Sophia said.

"That's where it was," Nina laughed.
"Thanks, Sophia! My teacher will
like the surprise."